Words She Couldn't Say

WORDS SHE COULDN'T SAY

A Collection of Poetry
N. Nevein

Charleston, SC
www.PalmettoPublishing.com

Words She Couldn't Say
Copyright © 2021 by N. Nevein

All rights reserved
No portion of this book may be reproduced, stored in a retrieval system, or transmitted in any form by any means–electronic, mechanical, photocopy, recording, or other–except for brief quotations in printed reviews, without prior permission of the author.

This book reflects the author's feelings and experiences over time. Some events and dialogues may have been condensed or recreated. Any similarity or likeness is a coincidence. These poems belong to the author and are the author's way of coping through therapeutic writing.

First Edition

ISBN: 978-1-63837-095-6

To my older sister, N. Thank you for opening the door of writing for me. It's your poetry that set me into a daydreamer's realm where creativity can flow through the ink of a pen. You helped me understand the importance of a beautiful notebook and a perfect pen. Pens choose the writer and we channel our own magic and creativity into those pens and onto our notebooks.

Table of Contents

Love Is...	1
Free to Love	3
Foolish Games	5
Just A Friend	7
02.06.08	9
Invisible	11
Conflicted	13
Conflicted Part II	17
Whirlwind	19
Untitled	23
Untitled 2	25
Abandoned	29
11.07.18 7:12pm	31
Cold Nights	34
Piece By Piece	36
New Year Same Shit	39
My Own Worse Enemy	41
Tunes Change	44
1.08.20 6pm	46
Science Broke My Heart	50
7:30pm	54
What's My Worth?	56
Cappuccino	59
I Went Out On A Date & All I Got Was His Autograph	61
Biggest Mistake	63
Fly Away	66
Burning Out	70
Disconnected	73
4 Days	76
07.24.2021 10:15pm	79
Daydreamer At Heart	83
She's Worthy	85

Love Is...

Love is blind
  Love is a fool
  Love was never kind
  Love is always cruel

Love put me through this shit
  Love put me through you
  Love is the reason
  That I'm broken in two

I'm sick of the word "love"
  What does it all mean?
  I guess it's all an emotion
  Of what defined you and me

I hate you so much
   I'm beginning to sound cheesy
   In reality, thoughts of you
   Make me feel queasy

This type of love was wrong from the very start
   I heard my instincts say
   That you would go and break my heart

Now that it's done
   And I found my clarity
   I finally realized
   This love was never meant for me…

Free to Love

I loved and lost you
   Now I'm living in a world so blue
   I couldn't tell you how I feel
   Now that you're gone, it's hard to deal
   That night you said those three words I wanted to hear
   But I couldn't say them back
   Because my heart was full of fear
   To express my feelings, a pen to the canvas to start the rhyming
   I know that we've never had the right timing
   Maybe in time we'll see
   That our love for each other can set us free

Love is truly wonderful if you peel back your layers and allow yourself to feel it.

Foolish Games

Love is not worth all this pain
   Love is not worth wasting my breath saying your name
   Love is not worth all these tears
   Love is not worth facing my darkest fears
   Love is not worth feeling ashamed
   Love is not worth taking all the blame

Our love is just never going to be the same

Fuck love! I'm over love's foolish game
   I've felt that way since you called me by her name

In this game, you played a big part
While I sat here and watched my heart break apart
The crying is over
The pain will eventually fade
Because of you, I got played by Love's dirty, little game

Just A Friend

Should I tell him how I feel?
How do I know if my feelings are truly real?
I see his face everyday
I hate that his smile has faded away
I wish that he could be happy
Even if it's not with me
I wish that he could see just how wonderful love can be
I want to see him laugh, not cry
I want him to stand and wipe his tears aside
He deserves so much better, it's true
I hope that my words can turn his gray skies blue

You'll have bad days, and that's okay. Give yourself time to feel it out. Then, push yourself forward.

02.06.08

I can't breathe
   I feel like something has a hold
   Out in the ocean, the waves pull me down
   I'm just me but it's not just me
   Nothing like you'd expect me to be
   Waves too rough, it's suffocating
   Hard to be myself while
   Trapped in her prison
   Her heart turned aside
   My stomach feels sick and I want to cry
   I just want to be happy, is that too much
to ask?
   Instead, I'm just hiding behind my mask
   I can only be me
   If you don't like it, then just set me free

There's an ongoing battle in my mind
   Who will win this war?
   Her or Her?

Invisible

You see me everyday
   But you pass right through
   With your smile
   With your glance
   I just wish you'd give me a chance
   I'm worthy of your heart
   But I'm just invisible

You talk about how happy she makes your every single day
   More and more, I feel miserable, wishing it was me
   But I'm just invisible

One day, she'll break your heart like the rest
   And I'll be here to clean up the mess
   No matter how many girls break you and leave you in the end
   I'm always going to be here, even if it's just as a friend
   I wish you can open your eyes and finally see me
   That one day, the girl of your dreams might actually be me
   But I'm just invisible

Just because you can't see me doesn't mean I'm not really here
   I'll wait for you until the end of time
   Until then, I'll just sit and unwind
   But I'm just invisible

Conflicted

Should I stay?
  Should I go?
  If I leave now
  Our friendship can be no more
  I could leave in peace
  You'll never know I'm gone
  You're too busy looking at her
  My flight leaves before dawn

Bags are packed
  Ticket in my hand
  As I walk out the door
  Behind it, you stand
  You tell me that you love me
  That I'm the one you want

I tell you that it's too late
And that it's not your fault
I should've told you how I felt from the very start
Now my heart is broken
And I'm falling apart

Life goes on and so will I
You're still my best friend
And that's no lie
I'll be here for you until the end of time
But until then, I still have to catch my flight
I grab my things and head out into the light

I hear an alarm and open my eyes
I woke up frightened and started to cry
It was just a dream, but it felt so real
From that moment, I had to tell you how I feel
I need to tell you that I love you
And we should be together

It might last a while or might last forever
We'll never know until we try
If we don't give it a shot now
We're gonna live with regrets and wonder "why?"

You can't see my scars
   They run so deep
   I had to cover them up with concealer
   As part of my daily routine

Conflicted Part II

I'm gone, no I'm not the one you're looking for…

Arrived at my destination
  Without you by my side
  The same scenario running through my mind
  Whether or not what I said was right

You finally realized we could be together
  And I answered back "not now, not ever…"
  Could it be?
  Am I finally over you?

I begin to unpack,
   Relax and unwind
   Until that silent moment
   When you cross my mind

You're outside my door
   Just like before
   Can't you see you're not the one I need anymore?
   I'm through with wanting you
   I'm just plain and simply done
   I just realized, you're not my special someone

This isn't love and it never will be
   You were just lost and on the rebound
   And the rebound is not gonna be me
   Back out the door you go, I see your back for the last time
   I need to focus on my own growth, just me, myself and I

Whirlwind

I feel irrational, emotional
  These thoughts in my head are like poison
  I need to look past the horizon
  And find a way to stay in control
  Why am I always the guy's girl
  Why can't I be part of a different world
  You've never seen me, just through me
  Only called when you wanted fuckery
  WE were never a guarantee
  I only wish this pain was something I could've foreseen
  Now here we are, here I am
  Standing alone while you continue your mind games

You never changed, always been the same

I should be considered so lucky to have a different mind frame

Yeah, maybe you're not to blame

It's my own fault—I should've known better

That's why I'm writing you this open letter

I learned a lot, I'm not perfect

But I know of my significance

I was selfless while you were selfish

It's what we were

A devil in disguise, a fool that rolled snake eyes

Thanks for making me feel invisible

I never really belonged

I had so much hope but this was never real love

I see a clear painting, what we had was a form of abuse

You love is like shades of purple, bright hues, baby blues

I hope you treat the next one like treasure, because no one deserves our toxicity
Love should feel like electricity
Passionate, wild, and free
Scars don't last forever, eventually this pain will fade
I'm ready to put my feelings out there,
This time I won't be afraid.

 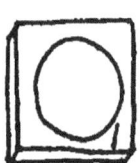

I wish I can tell you about this hurt
   But it's difficult to describe
   Comprehend my written words
   Anyway you want
   You won't get past the surface

Untitled

I missed out on falling in love for so many years
   All my heart did was yearn and weep
   I closed myself off and sat in the darkness
   No one should live like this
   It's time to change - it's okay to get hurt
   One day, there'll be someone that will treat me kindly
   The hardest thing to do is live stuck in one moment and to watch every one else move on and love freely
   Limbo is a bitch
   Letting yourself be free and fall is an adrenaline

Falling in love is no comparison
It's a rush, can take you by surprise
Fill your stomach with butterflies

Untitled 2

Words scar, actions are murder
  Just be honest, tell me your truth
  Tell me I'm nothing to you
  Trust me, it doesn't hurt
  I can turn my feelings off too
  Our expiration date was long past due

I'm not fragile, I can handle a few jabs & hooks
  It's your lies that felt like stabs and left me shook
  Build me up to break me down, it's your specialty
  Poisonous words dripped from your tongue lustily

Who taught you how to lie so compulsively?

I wish you could've fallen for me, as much as I fell for you
   Did you ever see the real me, or just someone you can screw?
   How many have there been?
   One, two? Must've been a few
   You can't be honest can you, it's impossible
   Your lies were so ridiculous, they were comical
   I was blinded, thought we'd be magical
   I couldn't accept that you weren't lovable
   Now I see what you see, our time together was laughable

Maybe one day you'll be moonstruck
   Only then, you can understand
   A love that'll feel like quicksand, you'll get caught up and self-destruct

How much will you be able to withstand?
Will you fight for it or let it be damned?

How long will you survive the inferno you inspired?
Sit down and pay attention
Learn how it feels to lose what you desire
Playing with someone's mind and heart will only add fuel to the wildfire
You're what inspired anger within
This blaze burning bright will never dim

You don't deserve any sympathy
You don't even deserve my pity
You couldn't see my feelings for you run deep

It's alright, I have no regrets
You're one less problem I gotta sweat
I'm as free as a bird, as beautiful as butterfly

Memories of you will blur as I'll spread my wings and soar the sky

You might have a disorder, you should get that checked out

Heal yourself overtime, learn what being human is all about

Abandoned

Why couldn't I see the red flags
   It's too late, you were wearing a mask
   We had a fun night together
   I was naive and fell for the empty promises
   Stop giving false hope, inflating fantasies
   This can't be my fault, I won't let it be
   I thought I could be myself with you
   A night filled with passion
   Followed by a day feeling abandoned
   What's wrong with living in the moment?
   Why are there rules to dating?
   When did wanting to fall in love become a game?

I keep saying "I'm done" and "I won't make the same mistake" but the cycle repeats with a different person. Like a washing machine, I'm stuck in the vicious cycle of rinse, spin, and repeat.

11.07.18 7:12pm

Fairytale mind games
  Making me insane
  Who made the rules?
  Why does the prince have to save the day?

Chance after chance, I haven't learned my lesson
  Why am I such a glutton for punishment
  You let me down, but I should've known
  You lack human emotion, you're like a stone
  I can't break through your barrier with affection

You had a tough exterior and I lacked the proper execution

Stay with me, even if it's just for one night
I just want your embrace under the stars and moonlight
Why is Love such a tough emotion to grasp?
Why is Love so easy to give but so hard to grab?
Why do I want something impossible to have?
Give me mercy, I need some guidance
My heart turned into fools gold
You lacked the touch of Midas

I wish you showed me your kind eyes and opened your heart
But I'm on the outside looking in, falling apart

When you feel like the moon, remember
the sun as it shines its light upon you.
Your beauty and significance will be seen
by the world.

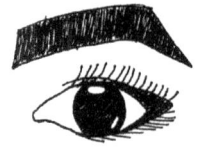

Cold Nights

Your mind games are driving me insane
   Changing personalities like night and day
   Leaving me with nothing but migraines

Walking away from you is all I can do
   When your mood changes as often as the moon

I look up to the stars in the sky
   Waiting for the cold air to dry
   The tears for the times you made me cry

You're light years away from allowing
yourself to feel love
   Because your heart is as cold as the
planet Mars

Piece By Piece

I find myself stuck
   On the ledge of a cliff, on the verge of tripping
   Piece by piece, a part of me goes missing

I hate that I'm the only one initiating conversations
   Days go by, you leave no words of reply
   Piece by piece, I'm left alone wondering "why?"

I gave you pieces in hopes you'd do the same
   We live with our own hurt, but chose to hurt each other anyway

Dating you is so confusing
Piece by piece, I'm the one losing

I look like a jigsaw puzzle
With many missing keys and locks
Piece by piece, my heart is enclosed in an icebox

Is this Fate's idea of entertainment?
My energy is running low and I can't focus
Piece by piece, being with you leaves me hopeless

I'm having some technical difficulties
saving myself.

New Year Same Shit

I'm the best woman you'll ever meet
   Vision out of focus, you couldn't see
   Just how far you've pushed me
   Your perspective of love is unreal

Sending me those texts
   Calling me "baby"
   What's the context?
   Do you want me? Yes, no, maybe?

It shouldn't be wrong for me to wonder
   What you're thinking
   Your intentions leave me pierced by thunder
   Pain so weighted, I'm going under

When you get what you want, you're available
When my questions get too deep, you become a ghost
Answers lost in a void
Work is the excuse you use the most

My Own Worse Enemy

I lose sleep over you and your empty promises
   Having nightmares of this person, my opposite
   What's worse, it's the person I've become
   Heartbreak, bitterness, disappointment, it's all made me numb
   I need to escape, I've gotta run
   I no longer feel safe under this sun
   The darkness is back and with a vengeance
   I feel it slipping away, my essence

Lost all confidence in myself
Overthinking every decision and I'm overwhelmed
Will this downward spiral ever end?
My saving grace, a therapy session with myself, this paper, and pen
Is the only thing I can depend on
Former me far from me, I'm losing this race
Everyday I'm playing a game of pretend
I wonder when the curtains will finally descend

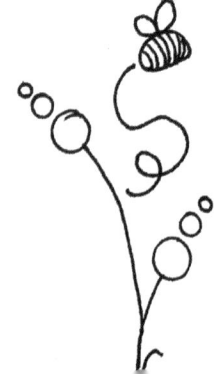

I'm always "winging it." I question if
I've made the right move. Each day, I'm
playing a new level in this game.

Tunes Change

I can't see you
   You're so far away
   The arrow went through
   Now I'm afraid
   The idea of love
   So bright and beautiful
   Seeing this blood
   Become a lustful disaster

You played me like a guitar
   The harmony within me is gone
   I need to retune my keys
   Learn a new melody
   Myself I'll have to work on

I'll be my own masterpiece
Soon you'll hear the music
But you'll never recognize it

1.08.20 6pm

Love is hard in the city of angels
   Trusted men full of betrayal
   Every obstacle is full of danger
   Every scar left behind is just as painful
   Watch me go downward this spiral
   Full disclosure…
   Falling for you was the worst mistake of all
   So tell me it's over
   And I'll move on

Fooled over and over again
   Just to hear "let's just be friends"
   Sacrificing my feelings just for one night

Just to read your text "you're a cool girl, but…"

To all the cowards I've given a chance

They remain in the shadows until I'm vulnerable and they're ready to advance

It's hard to accept that I've messed up by believing another set of lies

Heart on my sleeve, but no one will ever see me cry

I wish I never saw the potential

I wish I wasn't the woman that gave potential a chance

Unfortunately, mistakes are essential on this endless path of finding romance

I went on living without regret and now I'm regretting to ever have met you

I never wanted to forget until I wanted to forget you

I wanna undo the past

Or just remove the memories of us

If it wasn't you, it'd just be another recast

The pain of lost potential is inevitable
It leaves my heart with another deep cut
It's hard to get over the anger I feel
Even harder to forgive myself in order to heal

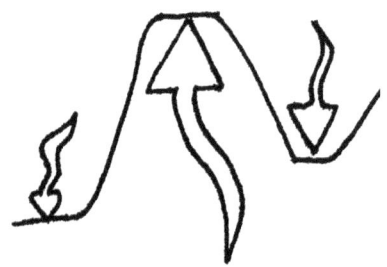

I see through your lies. You're not fooling anyone. It's only a matter of time before you're shut out like the rest.

Science Broke My Heart

I'm afraid to show my feelings
　If I tell you what's inside my heart,
　Will you stick around or run away?
　Let's be honest, my track record had a bad start
　I've been used and ignored date after date
　I wasted so much time on emotionally unavailable guys
　But being with you feels so right
　I feel it in the way you hold me at night
　The way you play with my hair and caress my face

In your arms, you make me feel safe
It's not just physical, but intellectual
So many topics we've discussed
Together, we're on a different level
So much in common but different interests
When my soul is drained, you lift my spirits
In your presence, it's just so comfortable
Whenever you text, I become vulnerable
You're so bright and positive, you further build my confidence

But I should've known, feeling so good would have its consequence
"Everything seems easy, our chemistry is lost in translation
You're great on paper, but we're missing the passion"
I should've slowed down before we collided
No one at fault, my fears come to life
Fearing the unknown, my heart's pulse is

the only sound
I opened up to you only to be rejected
Honesty you shared with me, I gotta respect it
In the end, you're still calling it quits
Because it just "didn't click"
I sit and replay that night in my head
I can't help but think of what your face looked like when those words were said
Soon, you'll be a distant memory
Your energy will fade away like many before
One more scar remains in this endless war of love
I thought that we'd be a piece of art
But Science came and broke my heart

Is the pain of being rejected over and over a waste of time? If I come across a similar situation down the road, will I stop, think, and make a different call?

7:30pm

It's lonely
  The day turns to night
  It's hard to breathe

It's lonely
  Your picture fades
  It's time to forget

Save me from myself
   Thoughts non-stop
   24/7
   Distract me from my own personal Hell

What's My Worth?

Why can't I find someone who'll cherish me as much as I do them?

Bits of my heart remain on my sleeve, tethered and torn

I continue to wear it over and over again

This journey to find someone special has many more miles to go, but my tank is near empty

I still often question "Am I worthy of love?"

Along with that doubt, I start to act petty

I know the answer is yes; while I do love

and cherish myself, I also want to share a different kind of love with someone special

The longer it takes to find that someone, the more that question remains in the back of my mind

The voice of doubt makes a strong case
Falling fast, falling alone
I'm pushed away with a heart of stone

Tempered and irrational
La La Land mellowed me out
That fiery temper was extinguished
Now replaced with doubt
Need to find my center and avoid the shame
Every situation I enter, it's all the same

I miss home. The city I was born in carries my heart and soul. There is no place that can compare to her, for she is a part that keeps me whole.

Cappuccino

A cup of cappuccino you made with warmth and pure heart
  Moved me to tears after the first sip
  While everything around me had fallen apart
  And I was starting to lose my grip
  I wanted to run and hide under a rock
  But this place, this person, this drink kept me from losing myself in the dark
  That first sip reminded me to stand tall and release the sadness
  The following sip reminded me to leave behind the madness
  The more I sip, the further I climbed upward

Silky, creamy, and light desire so warm
Your cup of cappuccino recovered my soul
And caught me in time from falling into the void
After that first sip, I gained control of what was being destroyed
Because your inviting smile, your technique
Made this cup of cappuccino unique
With powers to heal the sorrow and rid the anxiety
One sip ricocheted the arrow aiming for my sanity
A cup of cappuccino saved me that night
From the anguish caused by another and my overthinking mind

I Went Out On A Date & All I Got Was His Autograph

You picked me up at one
   As we arrived at the garden
   Full of greenery and light
   We enjoyed each other's company
   I had butterflies and felt bubbly
   I spotted an exotic beauty
   As you compared mine to a ruby
   We rested to enjoy the view
   You stole a kiss under the sun
   And made me swoon

Time spent with him feels incomplete
   I haven't heard from him in two weeks
   He left my messages on read
   But had plenty of time to send out tweets
   Went out and enjoyed each other's company
   At the end of the night, he made me feel like nothing more than a groupie

Just like the rest, he couldn't accept me as I am
   Because at the end of the night, all I got was his autograph

Biggest Mistake

Why do I even bother?

Thinking of what could've been, or worse
   Replaying the same mistakes over again
   Green eyes left me hypnotized
   A villain in disguise
   Swept me up into your waves
   And believed lies you weaved

Would you recognize me now?

An angel with so many faces
   Day and night, blinded by rage
   You were my biggest mistake
   Left on read, no reply

I wish I can tell you off
Let these haunting memories die
You're a ghost, can't be seen
A man with no feelings, like a machine

You try to manipulate the situation
   To convince me to stay
   All the while, you inched away the safety net
   So you can watch me fall

Fly Away

Is it hard to believe I'm the broken one?
   They fight and scream inside these four cracked walls
   In the end, I'm the one that can't love
   They're too busy working and stressing out over bills
   Escape to my daydream, where I have wings
   To escape the constant sadness
   This never ending bitterness
   Fly away to places far beyond
   Find a place of my own where I finally belong
   To a place I can finally call home

Your words hurt me, but I stayed silent.

My facial expressions can speak volumes.

I've been learning to love myself
   Some days are easy, some days are not
   The way I look, the words I say
   I question them constantly

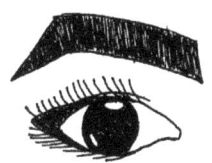

Burning Out

The stress of this job
   The lack of his love
   To top it all off
   Family is falling apart

Mental health is shattering
   Bottled up emotions are overflowing
   Fearing the unknown
   The negativity rapidly growing

It's not the time to breakdown
   It'll soon be over
   Stop these voices from shouting
   Inside, head is pounding

Pit of darkness deepens
   As the inner strength weakens
   Every night, losing sleep
   Every day, these eyes weep

Anxiety in high gear
   Fear has taken the wheel
   Mended heart is damaged and concealed
   Brain falsifying fantasy from real

It's not the time to breakdown
   It'll soon be over
   Find a way to hide this frown
   Tunnel light is getting closer

Words flowing so easily
  If I go back and reread what I wrote
  I'd erase every word anxiously

Disconnected

The feelings you reached are disconnected and no longer available
   Your feelings for me were afflicted and interchangeable

I get rejected, I hide away
   And become a stranger once again
   This vicious cycle of being ghosted over and over
   Each time, I think he might be the one, for sure
   Pulled my heart out let it hit the dirt
   Always piecing it back together, but it still hurts

After each challenge, another layer of myself is peeled away
   While this pain on my heart becomes too heavy to weigh
   I'm left more vulnerable and prone to heartache
   And I can't tell which persona is real or fake

I need to detach and go back to the drawing board
   I'm meant to be on this path of love alone
   Some people aren't meant to have another
   I'll be on that list of people romance won't discover

I wish we can be together
   Miles apart feels like light years
   Do you feel the same?
   Would you admit it?
   Or will your feelings be as cold as the night?

4 Days

4 days is all it took to crumble
   4 days for your mark to fade away
   It took 4 days to rip the rug from under
   After you convinced me you didn't want to separate

Presented false hope of you and I
   But once shit felt real, you decided to leave
   Made believe you were the good guy
   Convinced yourself with repeated lies you weaved

A coward hiding behind the word "yes"
   Pleasing everyone around you
   A ghost of a shell that does as he's told
   It's all you'll amount to

It's funny how you can hate the person
you once missed.

07.24.2021 10:15 pm

I feel fine when I'm left behind
   Another day, the world proves me right

I've come to terms, years ago, that I'm happy on my own
   Being by myself keeps me content, less confused, and secure
   I only started dating so I can test the world and my own fate
   I never sabotaged myself when I was with another
   Welcomed it with open arms and a compassionate heart
   But I was screwed over and over

I only pull away because I see the fall from the start
   Intentions slowly pivoting, their egos turning up a dial
   Fear setting in as their feelings for me couldn't be sustained
   There's a break in their brain
   They come to realization, it shatters
   They run so far away, over the hills
   A faded memory
   I'm still here, prideful as ever
   In an endless cycle of frustration
   Because the world and my fate couldn't prove me wrong
   I was destined to be on my own forever
   Not surprised, I knew it all along

It doesn't hurt me when someone walks away
   That doesn't mean I'm unlovable
   I love myself, and that's enough
   "Men" are just too troublesome

Maybe I'm jaded and numb to it all
   Because their rejection doesn't leave me disconcerted
   It's not worth it to cry
   Over the many men that keep wasting my time

All the men I once saw potential in,
   I can't even remember some of their names now

Daydreamer At Heart

I'm a dreamer
   That hangs her hopes on the stars

I don't want to stop daydreaming
   Escaping from reality helps me heal the scars

I'm still here
   I made it through
   All the bullshit
   All the heartache
   All the dysfunction
   I'm still here…

She's Worthy

She's worthy
  Of love,
  Of family,
  Of success.

Looking for chances, professionally and emotionally
  Lacking that special type of connection everyone talks about
  Feeling like she's disconnected from reality
  Or worse, like she's been the disappointment all along

Stuck in the shade, she stays optimistic
Even though a part of her is still pessimistic
Her pride kicks in and reminds her she's worthy
Despite all the pain, she made it this far on her journey
There's still quite a ways to go
Equipped with hustle and a sliver of hope
She realized she was never on this path alone

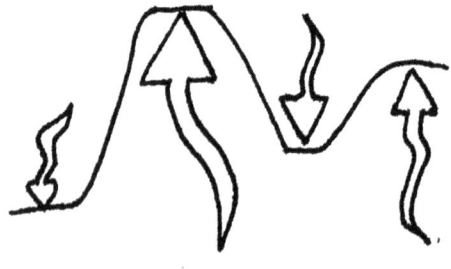

You matter, keep going…

www.ingramcontent.com/pod-product-compliance
Ingram Content Group UK Ltd.
Pitfield, Milton Keynes, MK11 3LW, UK
UKHW022234230426
12048UKWH00018BA/1254